Upside Down in the Dark

UPSIDE DOWN IN THE DARK

POEMS
Carol Potter

ALICE JAMES BOOKS
FARMINGTON, MAINE

ACKNOWLEDGMENTS

Dedicated to the women whose work, and words, and voices have made this book possible.

Poems in this collection appeared in the following journals:
Chester H. Jones National Poetry Awards: "The Cellist"
Field: "The Man at the Pompidou," "They Want Ice Cream the Color of Honeydew Melon," "Upside Down in the Rafters," "Cairns"
The Journal: "Trouble Rocking Back and Forth in Her Chair," "Digging to China," "Pay What You Weigh," "The Hanged Man," "Hey Baby, Baby," "The Summer After the Spring When Everything Flowered," "Pumpkin Pie"
New Letters: (Poetry Award 1990) "Golden Delicious," "From the Campground in North Truro," "The Trouble in the Third Floor Window," "Because the Egg Was a Door Nailed Shut," "A Round of Faces at the Dining Room Window," "Upside Down in the Dark" (originally titled "What the Sign Painter Was Thinking")
Sojourner: "In the Upstairs Window," "His Last Temptation"
Sexual Harassment: Women Speak Out: "Such Great Knockers"
Sexuality in Midlife and Beyond: Writing By Women: "Rituals"
The Women's Review of Books: "You Can Go Back Now," "The Catskill Snake Farm"

Epigram page 47: H.D., *Collected Poems 1912-1944.* Copyright © 1982 by the Estate of Hilda Doolittle. Reprinted by permission of New Directions Publishing Corporation.

With gratitude to Timothy Liu, Ted Deppe, Doug Anderson, Margaret Lloyd and Jan Freeman for assistance in shaping this book; Meme English, Joan Larkin, Pamela Stewart, Nina Newington, and Group 18 for support and inspired criticism; and to Mickie for her inspirational love.

The author wishes to express her gratitude to Yaddo for respite and generous support.

Alice James Books gratefully acknowledges support from the University of Maine at Farmington, the National Endowment for the Arts, and the Massachusetts Cultural Council, a state agency whose funds are recommended by the Governor, and appropriated by the State Legislature.

Alice James Books are published by
The Alice James Poetry Cooperative, Inc.
University of Maine at Farmington
98 Main St.
Farmington, Maine 04938

TABLE OF CONTENTS

Upside Down in the Dark

When the sign painter entered my friend,
I think he was thinking she would slide
open, would open up indefinitely but she was crying
out that it hurt, that he was
in too deep, that he was bumping up
against something inside her.
I was lying on the other side of the room
and I could hear her telling him to stop.
We were still girls, we were not yet
eighteen, and I listened wondering what might be
up there inside my friend. I didn't know
what to do, didn't know if I should stop them
or if it was pleasure.
Streetlights lit the room and I could see
the line the sign painter had painted on his wall.
He called it a water line
which would make you think there had been a flood
three stories up. I could hear them fucking
while the Beatles on the stereo sang, *You say*
you wanna revolution, well…we know, we all wanna
change the world which is what we thought we were doing two
years later running down Mass. Ave. smashing windows
and watching the store windows fall in on themselves.
There was a war going on.
Each night we watched it, saw the huts
on fire, the bodies in black bags.
We smacked the windows and each one of them
opened up, fell to the ground.
It was our world.
Around the corner the curtains in the bank
were on fire. There was a man in the upstairs window
looking out surprised to see us running down the street.
Inside me, my first daughter
tucked between my hips
swayed upside down in the dark as I ran.

The Man at the Pompidou

Sunning myself naked above the tips of two nails
which I did not notice
until I lifted my head
afraid I had heard some boat load of people
rowing into the cove, I sat up impressed
thinking I had achieved a state of grace,
become buoyant like the man I saw lie down
bare-bellied on a bed of crushed glass
outside the Pompidou Center.
Three men stood on his back
but he came up unscathed, just one small
scratch above his navel.
Inside the Pompidou, a nude was descending
a staircase, there was a piano score
with ants crawling out of it.
A blue cow was floating over Russia.
I was thinking the man's limbs must be hollow,
his whole body filled up with air.
I was thinking if I were to hold him up to my ear
I would hear nothing,
no chairs scraping back from the table,
no child at the piano practicing
his scales—
I hadn't noticed the nails, the tips
pressed close to my breasts
which made me think I had perhaps
learned the trick:
to be without weight. You forgive, you
forget as if you could
stick your head into the sky,
let the wind blow through,
clean out the house.
It was summer.
There were no human voices, no big boats
rowing into the cove.

My sister was on her way east
and I hadn't seen her since
last summer's argument.
What would I say to her?
She had told me to be quiet, the men
are talking, wait your turn.
I got up from the table
and she followed me out into the dark.
I keep telling myself to get through the meal,
you have to let things
slide off your back.
I was laying on the dock
looking at the smooth gloss of water
spread across the cove like glass
remembering how I tried to walk
on the storm glass windows
covering the family's cold frame,
certain the glass would hold me,
certain I was light enough
to walk on nothing, but I fell through
the window. Screaming, I rose out of that hole
in the ground, shards of glass
stuck in my skin.
The man at the Pompidou laughed;
he was working the crowd in French,
and I stared back wishing I had not wanted
to see blood.
He raised his arms above his head
triumphant, and we
cheered.

The Hanged Man

There is the love for it and the need
to rise above it, one of those strange
travelers pulling up to the lit
window, watching the family
quietly eating their dinner, then
pushing away as if the house
had been some shoreline no one
would set foot on. You are not the one
at the table, nor the one hovering
above it without wings, that strange sound
you make and the need to pretend
you can not hear. You let it
roll from your back, and you see her
walking toward you
down the road from the station.
You saw him, through the window,
put that metaphoric pillow
on her face, then
let her up in time
to breathe but you are not
her walking toward you with
her blue lips and those soft
fingers at your face, and you are not
the conductor of the south-bound train
coming down the track, headbeam
lighting up the lumberjack
hanging from the rafter
at the station, some kind of
talisman for loneliness; they say
he did it out of loneliness
though he had been working
in the woods with ten men
beside him. You are not
the ten men who had been working
with him, and you are not

him hanging at the station and he
never came into your room at night to lie down
on top of you and you are not
his hands all over you
in the dark and you are not
the train coming down the tracks
or the tracks beneath the train.
His loneliness was not your
loneliness and you are not
the loneliness that blew ragged
through him like the wind.

His Last Temptation

In the checkout line a young woman
was telling her friend about the fantasy
Christ was having on his cross: married
but celibate, she said he was fantasizing
about his wife. Nothing about how he
might get himself down
having carried his own cross
across town and up the hill
through the crowds. Nothing
about why if he could turn water
to wine and make bread fall
from the sky, why he could not
get himself down off that cross,
unpin the nails, heal the hole
in his side. He was dying of thirst
and the wind was there at his lips
but he would not make the rain fall
on his tongue.
In the house where I learned
about sex, there was a picture
of Jesus in each room.
I remember my friend telling me
where babies come from, how a man
makes love to a woman,
how he touches her breasts,
what he does inside her.
Jesus was on the wall, crown of thorns
on his head, blood dripping off him
but this look of rapture
in his eyes while my friend
showed me what to do with my hands,
and just exactly
where I ought to touch her.

Rituals

to L.

The set of knives in the stand,
a slot for each blade.
A woman is sharpening the blade.
I watch her, thinking of rituals,
of my father at the head
of the table and the rasp of knife
on metal, then the blade
cutting the meat. Delicate,
an easy slide against the grain.
She is sharpening the knife.
Is it the same knife
she pulled across her arm?
What happens in that moment
when a woman draws a blade
through her flesh, then disappears
with the arm in a bandage?
She found herself turning against
that ridge, hauled her wrist
along the point as if to test
the envelope of the body.
I ran my finger along that place
on her arm that she opened up
to the sky, that edge she leaned
against as if to give herself
more air, more light. Other places,
I wanted to tell her, people do this
to each other, the body with its lid
open to the air, faces hanging
on trees. Is this what happens
when love fails, slide the blade
across the wrapper to lay it open
like a present? She is sharpening
the blade. I watch her test it
against her thumb.

The View From Her Window

On the floor, the families wait.
Grief walks through their bodies, blossoms
at the end of each limb. There's nothing else
but this. It is like birth, how birthing
takes over the body, the one being born
and the one giving birth. It is like being stuck
inside a sack and the person trying to break out.
Where do they go when they go? And what of us
standing in the hallway, our people
in their separate rooms, tubes down their
throats, life support systems pumping?
They look like astronauts.
Where are you all sailing off to,
and what does that place
look like? We keep looking
at the view from my mother's window.
Such a beautiful city, we say,
rimmed by mountains, sunlight
glittering on the lake.
Her heart hasn't been working, the walls
flaccid, grown thin.
I sit beside her.
She asks me how I am.
I do not tell her
of my lover, this new woman
in my life. I don't mention
being in love. I keep staring
at my mother's heart-line
on the screen, thought I saw it
move the wrong way once, thought I saw
my mother's heart wave at me from her chest,
one hand flailing the air.

[handwritten in left margin: melancholy]

The Cellist

—for Adrianna Contino

At dusk, after being at the river
all day, she is playing for us, the cello
between her knees—It is part
of her body, and she draws the bow
across it swaying at perfect pitch
as if the air itself were moving through her.
Bach fills the room, and there is no
other sound but this
bow gliding across the body, and the music
from her fingers as it comes
gleaming into this room. It pools
around our bodies. We can see it shimmer
as it falls from one
rim to the next one down—
spilling until Diana plays it note by note back up
stream over those ridges off which we sometimes
fall. She is pulling the water back up to its source
where it swells for a moment in the cup
of her hands. I can see those notes holding
at the rim, a gloss of light
trembling before it comes
crescendo
through that hole in the heart
where the cello with its four strings sings, Diana
sliding her bow across it.

11

The Summer After the Spring
When Everything Flowered

It was the summer I had nothing left
to say. The wood thrush came
out of the woods, was singing right outside
my house. The sound pressed into each
room, four notes tied one
to the other, then the song
opening out into air.
It was July and the thread
of that song stretched from one room
into the next. It felt like desire
walking through me, reminding me
of the house I lived in two years
where the wood thrush sang, where she and I
thought we would love each other forever.
There is a thread through the body
and sometimes someone, something
pulls it. It was the summer it seemed
I was walking underwater, trying to make
way through milk-thick air, the wood thrush
singing incessantly. I found myself
thinking I should never have left her.
It was the summer after the spring
when everything flowered, each tree, each
bush. People kept saying
they had never seen
such a year for flowers.
There were white mouths
wide open at the top of each locust
and that sweet smell everywhere.
I had run out of words.
The flowers on all the trees stretched,
grew taller in the heat.
For one month I couldn't sleep.
Something inside me refused to lie down.

The wood thrush came to the edge
of the woods, pressed itself
against the window.
Each note was a bead on a string.
The bird pulled that string
through the house, these rooms
opening up inside me
the way a sailing ship inside a bottle
gets opened, its white sails
unfurled, something bright-white
blossoming. Beneath the glass,
you see the crew on deck,
completely occupied.

From the Campground in North Truro

Wind has been falling in and out of my tent all night long,
these sides flapping open, clamping shut.
I lie on the ground wondering how to live in this house tied

down with baling twine, stakes stuck in the sand,
neighbors on each side, three yards to the left, four
yards behind as if I was supposed to hear each story

they had to tell. What is it mocks us with its rash, that flies
after us because we are not yet god? In the dunes, the men,
making love, go down on their knees for each other

because there is this desire for some sort of
blessing, to be blessed in the hands of strangers.
Last night, from the people behind me, I heard how Jerry Garcia

recovered from his coma; his friend made him practice
delicate chord changes over and over until his mind
snapped back into focus, and it could make you think

there was sand inside the body and sometimes the sand
starts to slide. Why the heart walks off on its own, why
the body fails, and the heart walks. Bobby Dylan was singing

from their picnic table, *come in she said, I'll give
you shelter from the storm.* At one a.m., two men pitching
their tent to my left were talking about the man

who did not know the boy was a virgin. It was an encounter
at the bar, the boy dancing with his shirt half
open, his hand cupped at his crotch. How could anyone

have known? There is the soul inside which doesn't know
which part to inhabit, the heart walking off or the mind
inside the body with its rash because the skin

was left in the sun too long. This morning, two girls came
running to their parents, the older one complaining
that the younger one had been rolling

in the dirt again. In my tent, my friend was making love to me,
my head grazing the side of my tent, and my voice
wanting to go out into the campground singing

about *shelter from the storm.* You can look at the body, can name
marks on it, can recognize foot, hand, fingers
and the desire for some sort of blessing, to be taken in

completely the way the ocean can take us in, would have us
completely. It was that night I set my poncho on fire.
Too close to the lantern, it melted in a plume of smoke around

my body while I was trying to zip my tent shut. At dawn, a rooster
was screaming, and I woke thinking a child was in trouble.
A dog was barking. A woman shouted at the dog,

Get back in the yard, Derek. Derek went on barking.
The woman was arguing with a man. He screamed:
Drop it will you! She screamed back,

You brought it up, asshole! I came awake
thinking about my friend whose father
is dying of AIDS. When she was a girl, every night

she got up to check if he had come home.
I could see her, eight-years old, standing in the doorway
of her parent's bedroom watching her mother sleep,

her mother's breath like a thread ✓
through the house. She leaned in the doorway
listening for the sound of her father coming home.

Soon he will go and he won't come back.
There is too much we can't do anything about. There is
the question of entertainment. The question of the heart

and the way it pretends it can take it, can go on over
and over. In the tent at seven a.m., I was watching
light come back into the sky. I turned over

wondering how to inhabit this house, the wind coming in
hard off the ocean, blowing at us all day long
like we were dying for air.

In the Upstairs Window

for Judith

It was not all right when we got to your car and I saw the boxes
in the back seat, and you, laughing, asked me
did I want to go back to your house and help you pack.
You started talking about the weight of books, how much space
books take, how many boxes.
I want nothing to do with it.
Go home.
Pack it up.
Don't tell me it will still be the same.
There's a river through this landscape
and we ride away on it the way Cathy Fouloise's grandparents
rode their house downriver during the flood of '55,
the two of them in the upstairs window
waving good-bye. The front porch was stuck on shore
where the people stood watching
because there was nothing left they could do.
I keep wondering what it is we are all preparing for
going off to the new job in the next city—
It's difficult to refuse.
There's nobody to blame. You laugh assuring me
we will see each other even more than before.
Sometimes it seems we are each of us
under some kind of obligation
to learn how to walk away
as if we were all preparing for some grand
good-bye, the way it comes in the dreams I have
where the world ends and I stand in the field
watching bright blossoms flare on the horizon.
Looking across this distance, in the dream, I am
always wondering how much time we have.
There is a certain resignation
at that point, a strange new
silence, nothing more to be done.
I want nothing to do with this move.
This week, I read twenty books of poems

in manuscript: words, syllables, sound
on top of sound. You can hear it
on each page, something palpable,
the attempt to bring back
people gone, places forgotten.
Sometimes I think all we're trying to do
with these reams of paper
is to stuff the mouth of this world, to stave
it off—those two lips, night
and day, the sound of the word
good-bye.

You Can Go Back Now

This is the material you've got:
round, it's red and thick, malleable
in your hands, the size of a fist
and you don't want it. The way it
grows big in your belly like that baby
that didn't come. The one that got
itself started. A traveler.
Material. Matter. It doesn't
matter. It is the dream
you have of murder. In the dream you've
murdered someone and the police
are investigating.
Why did you go back to that town
where you did it, all the detectives
milling around? You're not going to tell.
They had you on the table and they had
your legs spread wide. Your marriage
was over. There were two others to feed.
It was self-defense you plead. It was
you or it, a him you think. The foot you see
poking out beneath the earthenware dam.
It's raining hard, and you hope the bones are
clean so no one can tell, no marks
on the body. It comes back in dreams,
over and over. Where do they go when we pry
our bodies open and unhook them, those odd
travelers in their strange blue suits
with the cord dangling?
Where do they go with their small
suitcases? You call your child
in for supper. Children trot toward you
across the playground, your daughter
and a little boy following, trying
to catch up. Someone thinks the little boy
is yours, calls out to your daughter:

Hey you forgot your little brother!
You think then he is coming back
to you, has finally found out
where you live. You think you should do something
to appease him. You put salt around
the house, sprinkle bread crumbs
on the sill. You see him feeding
at the feeder, his bright red wings
and that face you know so well.

Route 88 West

for my daughter

I am driving you 350 miles away from home
and I am going to leave you with strangers.
I am driving you into your next life,
and I am going to leave you there.
You are snoring while I drive;
I feel like shaking you awake. I would think
one might sit tall in her seat, memorize
each tree, each field, each farm. For hours
it's been one green field after another,
the silver tops of silos like blunt steeples.
What book is this in, Amy, which dream? Since when
am I simply supposed to take you places, turn
around, walk away? Exhausted, your lips move
in your sleep. I tell you
it's one strange town after another—
names I can't pronounce.

Latin

The Catskill Snake Farm

At night when she closed her eyes to sleep,
she saw snakes in piles, the way they curl
and twine on themselves. They were there

on the floor beside her bed. And when she
saw the neighbor's boy, John, wade into the
pen of snakes at the snake farm where he

worked, she felt her breath get short as if
one of them were in her lungs swimming or
perhaps coiled in her belly. He was wearing

tall leather boots. He bent down, seized
one large rattler, and held it up to show
its fangs. He demonstrated how they milked

the snakes, holding up the rattler, its
fangs like two white tubes and the white
milk coming out of them into the jar

he used for just that purpose. The fangs
were very long she could see and sharp.
She was certain if one of them bit you

it would stick in your skin and wouldn't
come out, just the snake hanging
off your body by its fangs, like Cleopatra

with the snake at her breast. It made her think
of the man in the barn when he called her
over to him one day and showed her

his penis. He made her let him rub it
on her and then she saw the white
pouring out of the end, like suds

she thought, and he told her she would die
if she told anyone what she had seen.
The semen was sticking to her skin. Some of it

had fallen on the floor. You might think something
could get spawned from that white pool
at her feet. She saw him put his penis back

in his pants. She saw him zip up his zipper.
She walked out of the barn blinking. It was so
bright outside, she could hardly see.

Upside Down in the Rafters

Squeezing through some crack in the house,
it came into my sleep and I woke to the sound
of furred wings flying through darkness, no
light in here at all, the way they like it, drawn
to absence and the steady breath of one woman
alone dreaming of a woman in a hospital bed
waiting for a prognosis, waiting for her name
to come up on the screen, and all those people
on the bridge watching three moons rise
knowing they were about to die, but still afraid
to kiss each other on the lips.
It was that kind of year, and me wondering
which gap in the trees
a person could disappear through.
I had no idea how I was going to get it
from the house, or how
I was supposed to live with it
upside down in the rafters.
Last night, on the pond, my daughter and I
sat in the canoe watching bats feed
around us, the thrum of insects
palpable, everything eating and being eaten
in the same stroke. The sun was gone
and the birds were up in their trees
with their beaks shut, but the black sky
was full of wings, bats snapping bugs
in midair then sweeping back up and around
as if to eat the dark between us.

Trouble Rocking Back and Forth in Her Chair

At a table with two men and five women,
the men were speaking and some of the women
were getting irritated because the men
were leaning back in their chairs, talking to the whole
table and everybody had to listen because
they couldn't get a word in edgewise, and I could feel
trouble starting to happen, the way I wanted
to overturn the table like the women did
at the bar in Worcester; one woman spilled
her drink wetting the other woman's
blouse so the woman with the wet blouse stood up
and stripped, making all the men at the table jump
backwards, five chairs crashing to the floor.
Everybody was irritated because the band was playing
its own music and the people wanted something they could
dance to; they wanted to get up and do the
twist, they wanted to do the monkey. I liked it,
liked seeing the chairs tip back and the whole room
get suddenly quiet. Trouble taking her blouse off
and everyone stunned just like I did it
when my sister was small, all that pounding
on the table and me shouting something
about the war. The men were talking at the table
and I was exchanging looks with the woman
across from me, neither one of us saying a word.
The other women were feeding the men their questions
and the men were answering slowly.
We just sat on it without a word because
we were guests there. It was the sitting on it,
trouble rocking back and forth in her chair
and saying nothing, made me think of my sister,
how she watched me rock and thump
through the house. They didn't like the clothes
I was wearing, and the brothers, I said,
were pinching me but we liked the way our sister giggled

when we chucked her into the air. Where did she go
and why don't I hear from her?
I don't like that I sat at the table without speaking
tonight but it really wasn't the right time to make
trouble. Trouble was something my sister didn't want
and who could blame her? She was the one
smiling; she wasn't the one I was trying to scare.
I think of the time I found her that day she got lost.
I was the one saw her come singing out of the woods, skunk cabbages
in her hands like nothing was the matter.
When I brought her back we were at the edge
of the lawn and saw our father come striding toward
us, shouting. She was screaming, digging into my legs,
shaking and squealing *don't let him spank me*
and I could not stop him and could not get our mother
to stop him. My sister dove behind me as if my rage
was some kind of skirt she could hide in, but he pulled her
from those folds without a hitch. I keep wondering if something
didn't get born that day. I think of the trapeze artists
in the picture I saw this afternoon, one man hanging by his
knees, his hands held out to the other one
coming flying off his swing to reach him. They were
both upside down with their hands almost touching
and the elephants in a line beneath them, the crowd
looking up. It made me think of her, as if
our fingers had simply touched in midair and nothing more.
In the picture one man flies through the air
forever poised at the edge of another man's hands.
In the picture there's no sign of trouble anywhere;
nobody gets caught, and nobody falls.

Cairns

These hills are full of rocks.
In the fields sometimes it looks
like they've been planted, stuck in the ground
on purpose like potatoes.
When I was a child, my brothers and I
rode the stone boat behind our father's tractor.
It was a long, flat, wooden barge
and we sat on it while someone
plucked boulders from the fields,
threw them onto the boat.
I remember the tractor noise
in front of us, rocks
accruing around our feet,
the smell of newly plowed soil.
How the field gleamed like a lake.
I remember the boat full
of boulders, but I don't remember
who was doing the work, or what we did
with the rocks after hauling them
from the field. Whatever it was
my father might have been building.
It was a strange crop, the boat
that would not float, and the children
piled up at one end.

A Round of Faces at the Dining Room Window

It was something she noticed
as she came down the stairs that evening.
It seemed the house
had blanched around some object
that just wasn't with them any longer.
She could almost put her hands on the shape.
It was this much tall
and that far wide.
She couldn't remember
how it was supposed to be.
There were people
in the dining room, a formal party
at the table. She looked in and saw them
looking out across the lake, the way
all the guests were settled
in one direction, their hands
gesturing toward the view.
Going outside to watch the sun
go down on the lake, she heard
the clink of forks on plates, some words
she couldn't quite understand.
She knew she was supposed to be
upstairs in bed, but she was fascinated
by the red light spread like long arms
shore to shore across the smooth
black eye which was the lake.
Turning back to the house, she saw
a round of faces at the dining room
window, the whole party
gathered as in a photograph, all of them
leaning toward the window, bone-white cups
in their hands.

Digging to China

In this story we are on a beach.
It is Sunday. There are people
on the breakwater fishing.
There are children digging to China.
You and I sit in the sand speaking of love:
how impossible when it goes, how terrifying
when it comes. You'd think love approaching
was an old man with a bell around his neck,
a beggar tugging at the blankets.
In this story the tide goes out steady
like pulling back a sheet so smooth
you'd think the water was on a cord
and someone was hauling it back
where it came from. The lifeguards
follow the water out as it goes.
We watch them in their orange suits
pushing their chairs toward the horizon.
Once again we tell our stories
of those lovers who once were
but are no longer.
Like flocks of birds they sit between us
and sing. Sometimes it is almost
impossible to touch each other
we are so full of this love
and don't love, this be here
and be gone.
There is a murmur on the beach, couples
turning in the sun, the white shock of gulls
wheeling and climbing above us all.
In this story, the ocean is a wide green river
pulling itself back toward
the edge of the earth gleaming.
It is Sunday.
The children are digging to China.
You can see their spoons shining in the sunlight.

The Trouble With Dolls

In the corner the doll is bright pink
with yellow hair.

The girl has given the doll
diseases: chicken

pox, polio, an undiagnosed
fever. She has cut the doll's hair

bald in small patches.
If you pry off the head

you can see the back of the blue eyes
staring outward. If you feed her milk,

she will start to stink. You can
throw her away, can separate arms and legs

from her body, watch rain
bead on her plastic skin.

Sometimes you see one
at the seashore, that nearly

bald head bobbing into shore, blue eyes
rusted open, staring at the sky

with that dark kind of patience
love sometimes requires.

Pay What You Weigh

The pregnant hostess was weighing the children
as they came through the door. You could almost
see the baby whirling in her belly she was
so far along. I could tell it had already been
a long day. She put tags on the children,
sent them to their tables. I watched them
being weighed and tagged as if the children
themselves were going to be part of the dinner:
Hansel and Gretel, a variation on Cronus popping
his suspicious children into his mouth.
But not here, the blond Boy Scouts shrill
were running between the tables.
They were waiting for their hamburgs, they were
waiting for Cokes and fries. They were waving
to each other and the small boy with the bad
voice, the kind of voice that works at a mother
all day long, was careening out of his chair.
Seconds later he was screaming by the exit sign,
stuck in a corner, squealing as if something
had finally gotten him. It made me think about
the other places where children
have been sorted out, this one to the left,
large one to the right, places where they are
right now being sorted. I don't know why
I can't just sit down, drink my drink and
eat my dinner. It was *pay what you weigh
night,* the restaurant full of children
running everywhere, laughing
as if they'd been promised that whatever happens
happens only in the privacy of one's
own home, someplace nobody else can see.

The Trouble in the Third-Floor Window

"He who troubles his household will inherit wind."
—Proverbs 11:29

Here comes the sun-spotted wind tapping through leaves;
it is the air in her mouth. The thread

through her body. It blows open the lungs.
Here is the wind, the sound of it

on her tongue, the wind across her body and her skin
that would inflate, would pick up and float

out of here, would lift her into air.
This is the wind in the vowel, the sound that comes

from her throat. She is the one calling from the third floor
window, and when you look up, you can see sunlight

glinting on her hands. She is the one in the window
waving, she is waving to you and the wind

seems to be stroking her body as she leans out.
Sometimes mother is drunk all day. Sister

has been eating too much and brother
has had his hands all over her. *Hey!* she yells

down to you on the street passing by.
Up here! Wind blows toward her

and she opens herself in the third floor window
hoping the wind passing over her will make a note

that will be absolute. She wants the wind to come into her
directly. She wants it to play her like a bottle.

They Want Ice Cream the Color
of Honeydew Melon

The sun this month has pulled itself closer to us or have we
gone out to meet it, changed
trajectory, gone out to greet it, pulling the blankets
back from our bodies? Tonight, in the park, ninety-six degrees
at nine p.m., the people somnolent, dazed, there is a man
with a sick child held to his chest. The boy is crying.
The man is walking the child back and around and forth not
knowing what to do, how to get him to stop crying.
· The child sticks to the man's wet skin.
There is a woman with a six-inch studded belt
cinched around her waist, bright blue leather
shoes, a miniskirt and her face pulled upwards by her hair
tethered at the top by a topknot.
A man with no shirt bends to her; he sits beneath her
on the steps. He wants something from her.
She is smiling as if she has forgotten
what she needs to forget.
She seems to be liking the weather.
She looks comfortable.
I think of the dream I had, holding a syringe of heroin
above my mouth, then drinking it, leaking the liquid
out of the needle and down my throat.
The heroin was the same color as the air tonight,
thick like milk but smelling of roses.
It would tamp the lungs shut.
It is some other kind of element, too sweet to eat.
It is a giant white poppy, a blanket
at our faces.
We would lie down in the park.
We would be nodding, our arms loose at our sides.
We would smile.
The man with no shirt is too fat, his flesh is wet.
He wants something from the woman, his belly
softening over his belt, jeans hanging low

from his hips.
I think he wants to climb into her.
I think he wants to slide down her throat,
to lie inside darkness.
To the left, three children climbing on each other
clamor they want ice cream,
they want the melon-colored ice cream.

Because the Egg Was a Door Nailed Shut

Here is the loon egg I found abandoned on its nest.
The loon had slid off its nest, slipped back

into the water leaving the egg
because the egg was a door nailed shut.

Here is the egg sitting on the window sill above the stove.
Here is the egg in the palm of my hand.

This is the smooth of its shell.
One gray stone.

Across the road you can see the trail into the woods.
You can see the woods filling themselves in, tamaracks

growing in one on top of the other, trails
closing over. I wanted to walk

back into these woods.
I wanted to forget.

Here is the spruce thicket, tight
like the palm of a hand held up: turn back,

go the other way.
These are the flow grounds.

You see the green grass swaying in sunlight.
You see the dark stream moving slowly through the swale.

A great blue heron rises off the stream,
disappears. How did you find me here?

This is the stream. I bend down.
This is the stream in the palm of my hand.

Here are my eyes.
Why did you come here?

The heron lifted into the sky.
There was no trace of it, no track

in the stream.
How did you find me?

I could have gone my whole life
without saying what I said to you.

Hey Baby, Baby

On the Common, it was March and the world
was lit, almost green, the budded trees
on the verge. The men on the benches
staggered as they stood; pigeons flicked
in circles around them. I walked quickly
by, heard a man calling out, *Hey baby,*
baby! to the entrance of the T where the vendor's
scarves flew straight out in the wind gusting
up Park Street. From over the hill, I could hear
demonstrators, that wash of voices rising
and dissolving as the wind shifted.
I descended into the green station, found everyone
on the platform listening to a man play
Bach on acoustic guitar. Some people were staring
at the tracks, some were looking
directly down the tunnel.
No one said a word.
When the train came and the doors
hissed open, we climbed into the cars, went
rocking through the tunnel, cradled
as we were in the dark.
I could hear the metal wheels
straining at the curves as the car
with lights dimming started to sway,
and when we hit the straightaway, we were
going fifty miles per hour. There could have been
another train parked in the tunnel, something
fallen in from above, a frozen
switch perhaps. I was staring
at the black windows, saw my own face
looking back at me, and for once
I wanted to congratulate us all, clap
each one of us on the back. How quiet
we are, flank to flank with strangers,
rocking and wheeling through the dark.

Such Great Knockers

Hey what knockers, what tits, just for fun, just for
fun they were yelling from the boat the two women
crouched in the surf, the man's hand on his cock

love, oh love, oh careless love he was singing in the boat
load of men come in close to see two women swimming naked in
the surf as close as they could come without

running up on shore his hand on his cock by the side
of the road he slowed down his car he called out
to the girl, hey you want to fuck he called

hey you want to fuck the boys are in the bushes
and they're playing a game with sister they invited her
to play with them they want her to be the wife, slut,

hussy, whore they will call her later for going
along with them you fat bitch you slut and some friend of her
brother's has invited her into the room to see

through the microscope so he lifts her slipping his
hands into her pants so she can look into the microscope
and brother is behind the door with his penis in his hand

and he is calling to sister come in please
he says I have to show you something I have to show you
something said the man in the barn this time

he wants to show her his pink penis standing up
in his hand don't tell anyone he tells her slowing his car
such great tits such great knockers hey baby you wanna fuck?

Golden Delicious

She was the queen's dream. The queen's dream
wore white gloves, carried an apple
in her hand.

The apple was too good to eat.
It was bright
and yellow

and perfectly formed. A Golden Delicious.
The white gloves
were too good to eat,

all ten fingers
absolutely
spotless.

Potato

One trusted family friend
who hired the boy
to work on his farm buggered
the boy who buggered his
brother who fucked their sister.
It was like some kind of game
of hot potato, pass it along,
telephone perhaps, instead the message
getting more and more clear
the further it goes and sister
standing there with the hot
potato in her hand wondering
what to do with it next planted
it quickly inside her body so
no one could see the blind
eye of the potato with its
white shoots sprouting out
from someplace inside her all
those new potatoes growing
from her belly her eyes her
mouth.

Nothing Complicated About That Kiss

Even though one of your other ex-lover's names
was on the corner of the blanket,
there was nothing complicated about the green
blanket in the sand, and the two of us on it.
It did not matter that we were no longer lovers.
We were "just friends" simply taking a nap
at the ocean, our faces tilted into the sunlight,
and then I kissed you. There was nothing
complicated about that kiss or you pulling me
over on top of you. Nothing complex about
being beneath the blue sleeping bag on top
of the green blanket and between your thighs.
There was nothing we needed to talk about.
I could see the pale blue of the sky above
your head as you rocked back and forth
on my hand, your cries lifting out of the dunes
into the murmur of the ocean
carrying your voice as you came.
It sounded like birds taking flight.
You cradled my face in your hands, pulled me
back to your mouth.
It was the first clear day of spring.
We slept under the blanket in the sunlight.

Night Swim

We were a chain of women, three generations
walking naked into the ocean.
No lights in the sky, no lights

on the beach—sister, daughters,
mother of mine, if there was never
another story to tell but that one night in August

we were a string of lights
bobbing in a dark ocean.
Waves dragged at the backs of our legs

as each black wall
pulled itself tall above us.
Holding hands, we dove

ten times
straight through
to the other side laughing,

delight and terror tipping our bodies
as we counted down the line
to make sure not one of us had slipped.

This is the story
that would like to go on
telling itself over and over.

Pumpkin Pie

It seemed there was someone staggering
on each street. Or was it the time of day?
The way light came in over the harbor
to slide around downtown.
It was the first day of spring
and someone stumbled on each street.
Or maybe it was just one man in front of me
catching his toe on the sidewalk.
He tripped and it seemed like the whole city
was tilting, built on a slant—
everybody fumbling in the spring light.
In front of Filene's, a man with blood
running out of his nose was shaking his fist
and screaming at a man across the street, *I am
not defeated, you fucking bastard!*
Fuck you, the man leaning from the curb
screamed back, *Asshole.*
It was the first day of spring.
All day long I'd been in the hotel
listening to writers read their writing.
A woman read a story about a woman with a knife
who slit her father neck to balls.
Cut off his dick, casual. Lit a fire,
casual. Blood running into the surf.
When the knives came out, I stayed
absolutely still. She was reading the story
and someone on the other side of the room
was laughing. Sado-masochism, free choice,
you might call it, a metaphor
for something larger. The woman
was reading, and I pictured her
standing over me, knife in her hand.
I stopped listening. Whose fingers
pressed my ears shut? *Don't say a word.*
Don't move. I stayed in my chair.

My friend walked out. I was reminded
of the story of three boys
shot in a field last week in Massachusetts.
Two were executed and the third
walked free. When the man was shooting, the boy
lay perfectly still. He didn't try to run.
The man thought he was already dead.
He put the barrel to the boy's head
and moved on. How did the boy keep his heart
from yammering, his breath like glass
from going in and out of his chest?
I picture him trying to press his
heart into the dirt like it was a bulb.
After the man left, the boy ran
out of the field and found
a street of houses. He knocked
on the first door of the first house
he came to, stood on the stoop
waiting for the door to swing open.
How do you start with a story like that?
The fictitious father was on fire,
the husband's nipples sliced through.
In the story the woman was baking
a pumpkin pie; she fucked herself
with the rolling pin. People clapped
at the end of the story, congratulated the writer
when she sat down. I left the room, walked out
of the hotel. On the street it seemed
everyone was staggering in the afternoon sun.
Fuck you, a man screamed
in front of Filene's.
Fuck you!

we crossed the charred portico,
passed through a frame—doorless—

entered a shrine; like a ghost,
we entered a house through a wall;

then still not knowing
whether (like the wall)

we were there or not-there,
we saw the tree flowering;

it was an ordinary tree
in an old garden-square.
                    —H.D., from *Trilogy*

We Want the Second Half to Be Comfortable

My teacher says that after the difficulty
of the first half of the word, we want
the second half to be comfortable, to roll
easily from the tongue. *Puerta, jardin...*
she says. *Watch my lips carefully;*
how I press my tongue to the back
of my teeth. I want her
to lay her hands on me, cure me of this
failure to understand much of anything
but what the dogs tell each other,
what the dogs want from me. On the way home
from class, practicing my r's, seven dogs
come barking and growling down the street,
two pausing mid-run to snarl and fight.
They had all seen something they needed.
We want to fuck, they snapped, scrambling
down the street, all of us
stepping aside to let them pass.
Later a group of solemn men
came walking slowly beating a drum.
At the corner, one of the men read a declaration.
I have no idea what that man said
anymore than I can understand
why my North American friend and I
are not speaking to each other now.
We talked and talked and told
whatever we wanted about our lives.
All of it. Now she's in the other room
and we hate each other. Nothing to say.
How we stand open-mouthed
whenever our first language fails.

Hotel Huerta

Beneath my window today, a woman
washes clothes in an outdoor
wash basin. Later, the girl
scrubs onions. Breakfast dishes.
Tonight the father is skinning a dog.
The daughter climbs up to watch him
disembowel the dog.
He has thrown the head over the wall
into the alley. He opens the inside
of the dog. There are two pups
wrapped in white sheaths.
He pulls the white membrane
off one pup, shows his daughter;
it is smaller than his palm.
He throws the pup over the wall,
pulls out liver, stomach, intestines.
Throws them over the wall.
The girl cups water in the bucket,
washes the inside of the carcass
as the father cuts.
He holds up his red hands.
She pours water over his hands,
rinses them clean. She is wearing
a T-shirt with the U.S. flag
on the front. Hollywood in block
letters printed across the top.
Her father's hands glisten
beneath my window.

A Woman in Her Cups

Last night, the woman riding
her broken heart around town, one wheel
half-true. Like the animals
in the hills, front legs hobbled,

that strange canter. I tried
hauling her home, in and out of cantinas.
Men were kissing her hand, they were so glad
to see her. I saw her take one man's

tequila from the table. He was watching
the singer sing, did not see her
unchipped nails at the base of his glass.
I thought I would make her safe,

but I left her drunk
at the table. Tonight the shore
of the lake is rimmed with gold-red light.
The sun has gone down, and the mountains

sink into a dark flush.
All morning I thought it was her
knocking at my door in her blonde hair.
I told my landlady, don't let anyone in.

Behind me, the moon slides into the sky.
Behind me, a man on a white horse
gallops a red horse at the end of a rope
up and down the pasture.

He is trying to train the red horse.
I can hear the pound of hooves,
and the bone-stuck-in-the-throat sound
of the red horse pulling against the rope.

Walking Past the Slaughterhouse

Two newly scrubbed pink pigs in full growth
appear at the top of the street, a man
with a stick slowly convincing them
toward the slaughterhouse, their cloven hooves
slipping on cobblestones.
It is the blood we saw gunneling out the back
of the house. You can't miss it on the way
into town unless you walk across the bridge
with your eyes shut.
But still there is the smell of it,
blood and shit dumping into the water.
It is the blood we step over
outside the house, empty cow skins
collapsed on the floor in the open door.
You can hear pigs screaming
when you walk by, the human sound
they make. On the way back from town
there was no sign of those two.
A man walked out of the house
carrying lungs, hearts,
livers hanging from a pole
across his shoulders, the wet weight
swinging at either end.
I stared at it, the trail he left.
As a child on the farm, I saw pigs die.
I know the sound they make, the sound
the knife makes popping through skin.
After the initial plunk, there's nothing
in the neck to keep the inside from falling
out. It comes out like a wave.
Who could imagine so much blood
in one body, the smell animals make before death?
How closely death rides beneath the skin.
All you have to do is open it up,
slide the blade in.

Once my brother made chickens without heads
fly from the apple tree.
I think of him up there
cutting off those heads—
such a strange flock.
Some kind of experiment
in resurrection.
How to cheat death.
How to live without the parts
you might ordinarily
need.

Day of the Dead

in memory of Barbara Brassor

The people are making confections
for the dead. Donkeys, chickens,
skeletons in coffins—

Day of the Dead. Day the dead come
walking to town to fill their faces
with sugar, booze. Smoke all they want.

Whatever it is the dead one liked,
the dead one gets. All week I have been
thinking of you, Barbara. I keep seeing people

who look like you. That winter
in your cabin, sunlight through the windows
beside your bed. How we craved the warmth.

Your hands on my back, and then the first soft touch
between my thighs. Forbidden it was.
Forbidden. Not to tell your lover.

Wild Turkey. Pot. Robert Cray singing,
You're such a bad influence, and the two of us laughing.
Here where I am now there is all this

sunlight, my legs tanned to the thighs
where the shorts stop. I stare at my legs,
this tan line, and remember the last day

I saw you. I held your hand, rubbed your
feet, your brown legs becoming white,
whiter toward the top. How is it

you tucked those hands and legs and went off
to the place you went to?
How could you be this much gone?

No Sign of Trouble

Today I saw the volcano I scared my sister with,
as if you could run down a street waving a volcano
over your head like a fat snake. Paricutín,
blue cup upside down, the inside of the earth
sticking up into the sky. It was the story
I scared her with. In the story
the farmer was plowing his field.
It was a cornfield like any other cornfield,
I told her. No sign of trouble anywhere.
He got to the end of the furrow, turned around,
saw smoke coming up out of the ground.
The ground had begun to boil.
He threw stones into the hole, but the hole
got bigger. Finally, I said, he simply tried
to stop it up with his breath; he was shouting
into the earth. By nightfall, the field
was a mountain, the villagers fleeing.
I described, in detail, people with flickers
of flame in their clothes, rivers of fire
chasing them. Ten towns buried by the end
of the night, everything turned to stone.
She'd ridden with our father plowing,
seen how deep plow blades slice open
sod, seen the dark inside the earth
gleam. I didn't mean to give my sister
nightmares. Our father on the tractor
after dark. We listened for the sound of him
coming home, the pound of his feet
on the flagstones outside the house.
Dinner dry like a bone.
It's a true story. You can see the story
carved on the wooden door in the village.
When you look up from the door,
you can see the blue cone stuck in the sky.

Dia de la Raza

In the bull ring, there was a circle of young girls
in white dresses, each girl holding a blue light bulb
in her hands waiting for the priest to finish his sermon,
the blessing of the lamb in the center eating a bale
of hay. I was afraid the lamb was going to be slaughtered,
the way it leaped around when the men tried to lead it
out of the circle onto the sawdust they had so carefully
raked. The priest went on talking, and then Mary came out
in her robe and an angel stood for half an hour with her

arms in the air. We were sitting watching with candles
in our hands. I didn't understand it was the birth of Christ
being celebrated until the angel had been standing
twenty minutes, the priest was still talking and the girls
dressed in white dresses like small brides stood still
the whole hour, blue light bulbs ready to light beneath
the full moon coming in and out of the clouds on Recreo

where last week two bulls had been killed, the crowd
calling out in the ring. Later, I saw them butchered,
hanging in the back of the truck outside on the street.
Neighbors complained of blood on the stones.

Refusing the Palm

Yesterday, in this heat, the reservoir
was like the flat blade of a knife
except for the man in the boat

rowing, one pelican swimming through
reeds, and three horses wading knee-deep
to drink. I watched them sink their muzzles

into the water, could hear them pulling
drink by drink up the sluice of their throats.
This morning, in the house beside me,

a girl is crying. She won't stop.
It sounds as if she is certain she has
the wrong mother. Wrong street.

Wrong country. She is screaming
in the corner of the yard.
I am in the kitchen washing clothes,

thinking of the three horses
swallowing the lake that looked like
the flat blade of a knife.

They wanted nothing to do with me.
Wanting only to stroke their necks,
I walked up to them

with my hand outstretched.
Ears flattened, tails twitching, they
turned their haunches, galloped from the reservoir.

These are horses that would not come
if they were called, lump of sugar in your hand.
All day you could stand in the field whistling.

Zero

There are so many people in town tonight,
the lights have blown. Candles burn
in the market, the tarps above the stalls

illuminated. I sit in my room, one candle
burning, and at the end of my leg,
swollen up and blue, the ankle I twisted.

I was watching the procession for the *Virgen
de la Salud*, wasn't watching where I was stepping,
didn't see the curb. Fifteen-foot high puppets

were coming toward me, empty arms swinging,
papier-mâché hands out of control, heavy like clubs.
They say if the Mayans hadn't invented zero,

all of modern arithmetic would have had to
await the invention of zero in the New World.
Hitting the pavement today in this town

where I know no one and can barely speak the language,
you could say I invented zero all over again
suddenly missing everyone I ever loved

in one flat slap of the heart. Flat on the cement,
I was full of forgiveness. You could call it
zero, the look on the face of the woman

standing in the doorway as I fell at her feet,
camera smacking the pavement. When I looked up to see
who had seen, she was simply staring down the street.

Cur

A brown dog picks through the ditch.
I am sitting in the shade by the side
of the ditch. A two-year old boy
throws a stone at the dog.
The boy has just been fed. He drives the dog
from the ditch, ancient balls
swinging between his thin hind legs.
These dogs are their own breed here, tooth
marks on their faces, torn ears.
No fat on these dogs. The bitches
pregnant or newly whelped, swollen sex
exposed; thick black rubbery dugs
hanging down, dried and cracked
from the sun. Sandpaper dogs,
dogs the color of wood, dirt
dogs. Bone dogs. When these dogs
die, they stay where they die.
You see them bloating by the side of the road.
The boy throws a stone, whacks the dog
hard in the ribs. Dog slides to the other
side of the road, into the sun
where no one sits. Comes back
disguised as dirt road, pile of sticks.
Sand. He lifts his leg, pisses.
The boy picks up a stone
larger than his hand, hits the dog
one more time. He doesn't want that dog
in his face, that pink tongue
at his lips. His mother has just
fed him. There's a white scrim of food
sticking to his face, wet stain
on his belly.
The woman and child get up, go
across the road, dog
following five houses behind.

Cabeza de Vaca

In the plaza, across the market,
a man from Canada is telling me
how to keep from getting sick.
Don't eat street food,
boil your water; be careful
with the fruit, he tells me.
A microbe could get into your mouth.
The head of a cow
stripped of its hide, perched
on a man's shoulder, is making its way
into the market. From where we sit,
we can see *cabeza de vaca*
riding above the crowd.
On the sidewalk in front of us,
a block of ice two feet tall
is melting in the sun—
translucent like a window.
This morning, in the Basilica,
a woman with a baby in her arms
came praying up the aisle
on her knees. I was afraid
of that woman's face, what she was
asking for. Another woman kneeling
in a pew was sobbing.
I was thinking about grief.
Garbage thrown from the bridge
dangling in the trees,
plastic bags fluttering like leaves.
Water you wouldn't wade in.
He tells me squeeze lime
on everything. Wash your hands
before you touch yourself
anywhere.

Daffy Duck

On the beach today, beneath the *palapa,*
a man selling plastic, puffed up
Daffy and Donald Ducks and 747's and beach
balls moved in and out of the tables.
No one was buying. A band was playing.
Charro music. Guitar, accordion, voice,
the musicians serenading the people
eating by the sea. Children were swinging
in hammocks strung between tables.
In front of us all, *azul* water,
coconut palms, fishermen throwing
nets into the surf. One man was asleep
in a hammock. The people started
dancing in the sand. The vendor
with the plastic Daffys and Donalds and Plutos
stood to the side squeaking his toys, idly,
one sharp squeal at a time.
He was watching the people singing and dancing,
watching another man finish a bottle of rum.
He was smiling, plastic bobbing in his hands,
squeaking as he pinched.
Later, on the beach, a man speaking English
wanted to sell me a condominium, the unfinished
structure behind us on the beach,
top three floors open, someone's laundry
waving in the sky. He invited me in.
For you, he said, *a Coca-Cola.*
For you, a swim in the pool.

Nightfall

It is nightfall, and the woman
outside my room
has been scolding a child
hour after hour
it seems, the voice
staccato, counter-
pointed by crickets
on stone walls.
Hers is a voice
you would lie down
in front of
because there is no use
moving. I want to lean
out the window,
scream at her to stop,
scream at the child
*run, and keep on
running.* What is it
makes us stand
inside the scold
and keep on standing?
Beneath my window,
a girl washes up after supper.
I can hear the cup dipping
into the cistern, water
splashing on cement, the clank
of dishes and spoons.
Bells sound in the black sky,
black sky filling up
with stars.
Radio playing, three houses
away, a man sings to the tune.
Te quiero mucho, he sings,
not quite on key.
I want you so much.

Woman Gathering Limes

Unwatched, he thinks, a boy cartwheels
through the neighborhood boxing ring
where last night two grown men fought

beneath the lights, the sound of fists
on flesh, men grunting, banging
against each other. I watch from my roof

as the boy spins three perfect
wheels, one elastic
leap into air bouncing himself back

off the ropes to land on his feet.
Behind the city, the sky is turning red.
A woman on the rooftop across from me

is picking limes, bending the tree
toward her, green fruit in her hands,
green fruit in the cup of her apron.

I have been thinking about happiness;
how we sometimes turn from it,
turn each other away from it—

that one pure note
rising from someone's throat
somewhere in the neighborhood.

Fer de Lances

Up the beach, dead coconut trees, the long,
tall brown stumps of them like something
beheaded. Stelae, a new kind
of antenna. Waiting for news
from wherever it may come.
Nothing comes but sky, clouds,
a flock of pelicans
three feet above the sea.
The snake most feared here
is the one that comes at night
to suck the breast of a nursing woman.
A man tells me the worst of it
is that after this happens,
the husband can no longer
sleep with the wife.
Once that mouth has been at her breast.
I picture her waking in her hammock,
bright marks around her nipples,
snake gone off in the moonlight,
mother's milk in its mouth.
Tonight, the crickets outside my window
are loud and shrill.
I have never heard crickets
like this before, and I think for a moment
it is snakes making that noise,
Fer de Lances leaning
against the house blowing
small whistles.
My friend says they look like
fat turds, but I like to think of them
decorated tonight in the half moon.
They are wearing headdresses
made of tinsel and tiny mirrors,
miniature whistles
gleaming between their teeth.

Bees

I sat down, Victoria said. *We started talking,*
and when we told each other what we were both
dreaming of, I fell in love.
When I met them, they had been in love two days

and he was oiling her body with coconut oil.
Already, she says, *we were trying to make a baby.*
All night long the hotel made of bamboo and thatch
pitched in the wind; the ocean 200 yards away,

waves bigger than waves I'd ever seen.
It was a hotel in the sand, a kitchen
in sand. I watched them walking
naked hand in hand into the surf, and when she left

for the mountains to meet his family, I said to her,
You have to write to me. I want to know
what happens. I want to know what it means
to step through a door and fall in love

knowing full well how love fails, that fracture
everywhere. On the street here, girls sell
homemade sweets: fudge, peanut
brittle, red blocks of jelled

guava. The girls who sell sweets
sit in the midst of bees. Honey bees
indolent on the fudge, honey bees
stuck in guava. Wind picks up the corners

of the cellophane covers,
bees squeeze through the gaps.
They walk across the macaroons;
they swarm across the sweet.

Ice Cream on the Beach

Like in a dream, after dragging me
out to sea, finally the undertow has let me
go, and I'm bobbing too far from shore to break,
wondering if I should call out
to people baking themselves in the sand,
if they would hear me if I called.
Like in a dream, I tell myself *stay calm.*
You can float if you need to.
How quiet it is out here beyond the breaking.
There's a half moon in the sky, people
turning themselves in the sun, and a young man
selling ice cream. He's pushing the cart
up the sand slowly, metal box
on wheelbarrow, metal wheel
sinking into the sand.
It is hot on the beach, too hot
to walk barefoot.
From where I float, I remember the heat,
hot sun like a nail on my head.
A woman with bare breasts
walks toward the man selling ice cream.
This is the ice cream on the beach dream.
This is the palm fronds waving in a cobalt sky dream.
From the swell of a large wave
forming, I see the woman with bare breasts
lean over the ice cream cart.
She is trying to decide which flavor she needs.
Like in a dream, I feel the cold air of ice cream
touching each nipple like a tongue.

Fourth Day of Wind

I can imagine wanting
to tape the wind shut, that great mouth
wide open and blowing. There's a fine

dust on everything. Palm trees rattle,
bamboo fences buzz in the wind.
Somehow, the soft green tops of onion manage

to stand. In the wind, men and women on shore
clean and group onions, pack them in the shade
of the palapa, talking softly. On a table,

in the dust from the wind, a woman is cutting
onions. The restaurant is half full, people
staring at the lake wondering when the wind

will stop. Last night, in the wind,
a woman I didn't know appeared
in my room, drifted through the open door

toward the light. She sat down on my bed.
I asked her if she was all right. She stared at me,
repeated her name, and would not

move. This morning the wind
is like someone who won't stop
talking, that voice across vertical fields.

This wind in and out of our faces, our hands,
our eyes. As if to teach us another way to breathe.
What to do when there's nothing in the world but air.

The Big Dogs Barking

The small dog, Misha, is sleeping now, resting
from his barking. The black and white fur
too hot in the day but good at night
for running back and forth in the sand all
those short retorts under the stars.
Good for waking whomever he can.
The woman next door, the one who
needs her head next to the ocean in order to sleep.
Something to drown the human voices, and the dog
barking. She needs her ears
pressed tight to the current.
At night Misha runs up and down his yard
on his dog-short legs barking.
There is something coming over the hill
he needs to address, the big dogs barking.
He's seen them on the beach, the pack
they run in. What they say to each other
chasing joggers, how they jump and roll
and fuck together, sleep out beneath the stars.
They get food and water wherever they find it,
loose wrappers on the beach, unattended dish
water, a toilet left open.
When the big dogs bark, the small one
yells something at them from his yard—
he has people, his people have a restaurant,
a boy who throws sand at him.
The boy he follows on the beach, the boy
whose bed he wants to sleep in.

Going Home

It was an impossible act:
suicidal, the man diving

from the top of the *cenadora*
into the stream

sixty feet below. The stream
did not look deep enough

to contain a man
diving from the sky,

but he entered the water
precisely where he needed.

It takes a good eye,
some sort of instinct

in the body.
The wind just right.

They Wanted A Woman to Dance With

I was the only woman on the boat
and the soccer team from Aguascalientes
was dancing.
They wanted me to join
but I sat in the stern,
watching the men
waltz each other.
I was too embarassed
to dance, the pitch
of the boat, the arms
of the men watching.
In my house now, small brown
moths have become familiar as air.
They fly through the evening light
shimmering off the lake
onto the walls of the house.
I was thinking of the band
on the boat,
how I could barely hear it
above the motor.
How the men were laughing.
They wanted a woman
to dance with.
When the moths fly up,
I cannot hear their
wings, the small brown
of their bodies.
In certain hours of the evening,
they become beautiful.

To Gail in Pátzcuaro

⌘

We watched them light candles,
kneeling to a god
we can't name.
Everywhere you and I went,
it was someone else's home,
which is what I thought was true—
that there is no home,
nowhere a person
is not alone.
I thought you could teach me to love it.
That night on the hotel roof,
I wanted to kiss you but I didn't.
Elastic stars, elastic moon
diving in and out of white clouds.
Behind us, white sheets shook
on the clothes line, and we could hear
a mariachi band up the street.
When I went to bed, I listened
to the city disappearing
one layer of sound at a time
until finally all I could hear
was you in the next room, coughing.

⌘

After I returned, my grandmother
was put in a nursing home.
I loved telling you her story,
how she walked the beach
every day at ninety-three, that the women
in my family don't falter.
The truth is we want the halt
and lame to belong to someone
else.
We want them walking

so far ahead
we lose sight of them.
My grandfather in the woods,
my aunt as a little girl
watching the heels of his boots
disappearing around the far bend
out of sight; she couldn't
keep up.
Then he left the family,
died someplace else.

You want to know how it's been for me.
Reentry we call it, coming home.
A woman keeps telling me it's like
I haven't yet returned.
I think of that last afternoon with you
on your porch; we'd been drinking rum,
smoking, and Don was talking
about what was wrong in the States.
No mystery he said, no sense
of the sacred.
He told us about his love life,
what she'd said to him, what he'd said
to her. The color of her nail
polish, the pointy high heels she wore
everywhere she went.
She made me crazy, he said.

After Long Drought

Last night, the oldest living member of my family
went running up and down the halls
of the rest home naked. *There's no*
soothing me, she says. *You can't*
comfort me, there's no use trying.
It rains here, it rains day after day.
It is late September now
and no one asks me what it is like
to be back. I should tell you.
What the earth upriver has sloughed off
comes past me. Logs, grass, pieces of earth.
It is rapid now, the slippage,
what goes and does not come back.
I think of what I left behind, how I am
not where I want to be
no matter which way I face on this river.
What we get here is the tenderness
of rain, the river comes back
from the ocean, climbs into the sky
and blows inland on us.
That tenderness. As after long drought,
my brother and I stood with our father
in the doorway of the barn watching
the rain come. The fields planted in corn
were powder. The drops of rain
thudded into the powder at our feet.
My brother and I danced and jumped
in the rain in front of our father
who was looking away from us
at something else.